SKYDIVE

SKYDIVE

Kevin Kerr

Talonbooks

Talonbooks
Box 2076, Vancouver, British Columbia, Canada V6B 3S3
www.talonbooks.com

Typeset in Adobe Garamond and printed and bound in Canada.
Printed on 100% post-consumer recycled paper.

First Printing: 2010

The publisher gratefully acknowledges the financial support of the Canada Council for the Arts; the Government of Canada through the Book Publishing Industry Development Program; and the Province of British Columbia through the British Columbia Arts Council and the Book Publishing Tax Credit for our publishing activities.

Library and Archives Canada Cataloguing in Publication

Kerr, Kevin, 1968–
Skydive / Kevin Kerr.

A play.
ISBN 978-0-88922-638-8

I. Title.

PS8571.E719S59 2010   C812'.6   C2009-906978-4

For Bob and James
and
In loving memory of Azra North Young (1995–2009)

Acknowledgements

The playwright wishes to thank the following people and organizations for their generous support in the development of *Skydive*:

James Sanders, Bob Frazer, Realwheels Theatre, The Canada Council for the Arts, Sven Johansson, Roy Surette, Stephen Drover, The Belfry Theatre, PuSh International Performing Arts Festival, The Banff Playwrights Colony (2006), Maureen Labonte, Dennis Garnhum, Shari Wattling, Theatre Calgary's FUSE play development program, The Vancouver Playhouse Writer-in-Residence Program, The Lee Playwright-in-Residence program at the University of Alberta's Department of Drama, Marita Dachsel, and Azra Young for her encouraging words and friendship.

The Origins

Skydive was a commissioned work, but unlike any commission that I had encountered before or since. It started with a phone call in late 2003 from my friend, former classmate, and very gifted actor, Bob Frazer. He was soliciting playwrights to submit suggestions for a new play to feature him and his long-time friend and fellow artist, James Sanders.

James was in the process of forming a theatre company which had as part of its mandate providing opportunities for professional artists with disabilities and increasing the audience's understanding of the disability experience. James happens to be a quadriplegic as a result of an injury that interrupted his theatre training at Douglas College in New Westminster, where he had first met Bob. After a period of rehab, he continued with his training as an actor, eventually graduating from Simon Fraser University's theatre program. Also in that time, Bob and James became much closer friends and keen advocates of each other's work.

When I met with them to talk, James explained that he wanted to go beyond the issue of disability as story, which he felt had been done a fair bit already. James spoke of normalizing disability for an audience by presenting theatre where the physicality of the actor is incidental to the story. He wanted to present work that engaged the audience with great narratives, spectacular staging, and powerful acting, and in which one character/actor might happen to use a wheelchair for their method of mobility in the same way another character/actor might happen to be blonde. You don't deny the physicality, you just don't make it the point. You hope the audience gets lost in the story and the physicality drifts further and further into the background until it's just another given in the overall performance. This excited me.

As I listened to James and Bob's conversation, I was struck by the extraordinary relationship between the two men. Theirs is a story of grabbing hold of one's destiny; of embracing the unknown in pursuit of growth, understanding, and adventure; of looking fear in the face and staring it down; being able to laugh at oneself while mercilessly ridiculing the other. And I knew no matter what else the play turned out to be, the core of it was right in front of me in this no-holds-barred friendship.

The Legend

Skydive had its true beginnings at the Ivanhoe, a seedy bar in Vancouver's downtown eastside. The three of us began to hold regular "work meetings" there to begin imagining the possibilities for the play and review various scenarios and scene ideas that I would pitch to them. On one fateful night after a few inspirational, and I think entirely tax-deductible, beers, Bob was ranting about conventions in theatre and how he was tired of going to plays and, in the darkness before the lights first came up, detecting actors sneaking into position for their first scenes. He wanted to be surprised, be unaware of where the actors were coming from or where they would be when the play began. And then, in a passionate and fateful outburst, threw his arms in the air and said, "Wouldn't it be awesome if the play began with the actors falling from the grid?" Stunned silence from James and me. True, no one would expect that. James shifted in his chair and we exchanged smiles that translated to, "Okay, Bob's cut off," and we went on to other topics.

But at our next meeting, I told them that I hadn't been able to stop thinking about the image of the two men falling through space. The impossibility of the image and the excitement that it provoked stuck with me and I wanted to know how we could do it. At that moment, James revealed that he had recently got to know Sven Johansson, a Victoria-based, self-described aerial choreographer, who had devised something he called ES Dance Instruments, which enabled dancers to fly onstage. I had seen Sven's work onstage in a couple of plays where the instruments were employed as special effects for brief moments in a show and knew that they provided unbelievable, jaw-dropping images and movement unlike anything normally seen on stage. At this moment, *Skydive* was truly conceived; when James contacted Sven who agreed to collaborate with some experimental workshops to see if he could help a quadriplegic fly, the vision of a play that took place entirely in the air began to materialize.

The Technology

The ES Dance Instrument is essentially a long pole on a fulcrum, like a giant teeter-totter. Traditionally (if you can use that word to describe such an innovative device), a dancer sits on a bicycle seat at one end and is secured with a belt around the waist. At the other end is a counterweighted wheel controlled by an operator. The dancer can then be lifted vertically in the air as high as seventeen feet, be flown left and right along the horizontal plane, spun 360 degrees in a cartwheel motion, and pivoted to face left or right in profile to the audience (and thereby turning the cartwheels into somersaults and back-flips). The entire instrument can also be tracked up and down stage allowing for the performer to occupy almost any point in the space above the stage and in almost any position. With two performers, each in an instrument, the potential for physical composition became almost limitless.

To accommodate James's unique physicality, some modifications had to be made. A series of braces were developed by experts in orthotics at Vancouver's GF Strong Rehabilitation Centre, who eventually created a fiberglass shell cast to fit James's legs and torso, which was then affixed to the instrument. James could then fly in the instrument with his body being supported in a standing position and able to experience the full range of motion of the ES Dance Instrument. Thus the bodies of both performers, each with very different physicalities, were essentially equalized. And what I found to be particularly compelling was that by way of this technology they were liberated to move in ways that none of us able-bodied or otherwise could ever dream of, while at the same time they were restrained and dependent entirely upon the actions of the operators. It was an image that spoke to me of the limits we all face as physical beings forever trapped in our fragile and imperfect bodies, as well as the boundless nature of our imaginations and dreams and the constant attempts we as humans make to exceed our earthbound restraints.

The Collaboration

Skydive was created as a fluid collaboration between text, actor, choreography, design, technology, and staging. We conducted a number of workshops with Sven and his ES Dance Instruments to first test our hypothesis that we could

James Sanders and Bob Frazer in performance.
Actors appear courtesy Canadian Actors' Equity Association.

Photo: Tim Matheson

have two actors suspended above the stage for a ninety-minute show. After that proved possible, we worked with the instruments to inform the story and action of the piece and to explore the imagistic possibilities provided by the unique physicality available with this technology. With the addition of co-directors Roy Surette and Stephen Drover, the play was developed with a dramaturgy based in movement, image, and physicality as much as it was in the usual questions of narrative, character, and story. Continually fuelled by both the chemistry of the actors and the spectacle of their bodies in flight, scenes would suggest themselves and then arrive through a fusion with my own questions about fear, relationships, loss, and the power of dreams in our lives.

The result was a piece that I feel is a testament to the collaborative nature of theatre as well as to the energy and spirit of two of the most inspiring individuals I've had the pleasure to know.

SKYDIVE

Skydive was created by Realwheels (Vancouver, BC) and developed in association with the Belfry Theatre (Victoria, BC) and Theatre Calgary's FUSE Play Development Program. The premiere production of *Skydive* was commissioned by the PuSh International Performing Arts Festival and was co-presented by Realwheels and PuSh in Vancouver, BC, on January 26, 2007, with the following company:

MORGAN: *James Sanders*
DANIEL: *Bob Frazer*

Operators: *James Dahl, Jethelo E. Cabilete, Christopher Frary, Lee Vincent*
Directed by: *Roy Surette, Stephen Drover*
Aerial Choreography: *Sven Johansson*
Set Design: *Yvan Morissette*
Lighting Design: *Adrian Muir*
Costume Design: *Keith A. Parent*
Sound Design: *Alessandro Juliani, Meg Roe*
Props: *Tracy Lynch*
Stage Manager: *Angela Beaulieu*
Production Manager: *James Pollard*

A revised version of the play premiered October 16, 2008, at Theatre Calgary, with the original artistic team except for the addition of Shane Snow, who performed as an operator in place of James Dahl. ·

Characters

MORGAN: 30s, an enthusiast
DANIEL: 30s, a recluse

A Note on Language and Music

Morgan often mispronounces or confuses words, saying things like "agrophobia" for "agoraphobia" or pronouncing "pilates " as "pie-lates." He's generally
unapologetic and speaks with an entirely unearned authority.

Music played a big part of the original production, with popular tunes
from the 1980s forming a sort of soundtrack of nostalgia for the two men. In
a couple of passages, specific songs played a central role in the action of the
scene, with the characters lip-synching or singing the familiar tunes.

THE JUMP

Wind. The sound of plane roaring by. Music. '80s metal. Loud! Lights up as MORGAN and DANIEL plummet from the grid with screams of delight.

The men have parachutes strapped to their backs and their costumes billow around them in the wind as they free-fall.

A series of well-executed free-falling positions: the delta, the spread stable, the stable back to Earth, the vector.

After a little more free-flying, the guys attempt a little trick of coming together and grabbing hands. They struggle against the overpowering wind resistance in their free-fall. Their fingers extend, extend, a momentary image of God reaching out for man with the spark of life, then stretching, stretching, stretching and so close, but no contact, and then.

MORGAN checks his altimeter. He gives the thumbs up sign and the two men reach for their ripcords. As they look at each other, DANIEL pulls his cord. Nothing happens. He pulls again and something tears off in his hand. Fear grows on his face and he desperately looks to MORGAN for some sort of assistance. MORGAN looks at DANIEL helplessly and then pulls his own ripcord. His chute deploys and the two men separate as MORGAN slows down and DANIEL plummets towards the earth.

Shift.

THERAPY

In the darkness, a whisper:

DANIEL: Wake up.

Mom's house, evening. New age relaxation music plays softly. DANIEL lies on his back; MORGAN sits and takes notes.

MORGAN: So, Daniel, how have you been sleeping?

DANIEL: I keep having weird dreams.

MORGAN: Yes.

DANIEL: You know?

MORGAN: Go on.

DANIEL: Last night I dreamt I was … falling.

MORGAN: Mmm-hmm.

DANIEL: This is strange.

MORGAN: I hear it all the time.

DANIEL: Not the dream. This. I don't feel comfortable with this "therapy" thing.

MORGAN: That's your fear talking.

DANIEL: No, it's me talking about being not too sure that I like the idea of doing this with you.

MORGAN: Why not?

DANIEL: Because you're my brother.

MORGAN: I see. (*He makes a note.*) Do you want to tell me about your childhood?

DANIEL: No.

MORGAN: Why?

DANIEL: You were there. This is the point. You can't be objective as my therapist, and I can't be relaxed. We should stop now.

MORGAN: You've still got fifteen minutes by my watch. And I charge by the hour.

DANIEL: Well, keep the change.

MORGAN: Interesting choice of words: "Keep the change."

DANIEL: God, Morgan. Really?

MORGAN: Your cynicism is just a defence. Acknowledge and move through.

DANIEL: Who are you? Where's all this coming from, Morgan?

MORGAN: My heart.

DANIEL: I think the location's a little farther south and back a bit.

MORGAN: I'm just trying to create a mood, a safe environment.

DANIEL: Morgan, you're not a legitimate counsellor.

MORGAN: Daniel, I have several clients.

DANIEL: You don't have a licence.

MORGAN: What are you talking about? Of course I do.

DANIEL: You have a "Serving It Right" certificate and a table at the Farmer's Market. You're not a registered therapist.

MORGAN: You know Freud didn't have a "licence."

DANIEL: I believe he had at least a medical background.

MORGAN: Medical backgrounds. You can't teach a person how to be a good listener.

DANIEL: Well, actually, Morgan, I think—

MORGAN: Just shut up for a second. A person is either a born listener or he's not. Freud's success was not his medical background; it was the fact he could listen and inspire trust. And the women would feel free to tell him their deepest secrets.

DANIEL: Right.

MORGAN: That, and he would routinely get them off with a vibrator. That's the origin of the whole lie on the couch business; did you know that? End of the session: "One more thing." Up goes the dress and *buzzzzz*. "Oh, thank you, doctor, I am feeling better about myself." Sometimes a cigar is just a cigar, but other times … eh?

DANIEL: You've totally lost me.

MORGAN: What?

DANIEL: What are talking about?

MORGAN: About helping you?

DANIEL: I thought this was you practising your new "career."

MORGAN: Mom called me.

DANIEL: Mom?

MORGAN: She told me you needed help.

DANIEL: She called you?

MORGAN: Yeah, three in the morning. Was a bit creepy, her voice was all … garbly. But she said you were stuck in here, and I should come.

DANIEL: You sure it wasn't a dream?

MORGAN: No it wasn't. It was pretty specific. She said she hadn't seen you for a long time.

DANIEL: It's just that Mom isn't really making any phone calls lately.

MORGAN: What do you mean?

DANIEL: Well, she's not often lucid. The drugs and things. You might know that if you ever visited or called or—

MORGAN: I sent her a get well card.

DANIEL: Oh, that's very thoughtful, Morgan. She's not going to get well.

MORGAN: Negative thinking.

DANIEL: Facing reality is not negative thinking.

MORGAN: And you're facing reality by hiding out in Mom's house?

DANIEL: No, I'm not. I want out. I feel terrible, I haven't visited Mom in weeks because of this, and it kills me to think of her in that home all by herself.

MORGAN: Hey, I said I sent her a card.

DANIEL: That's not what I mean. I'm just saying I'm trapped.

MORGAN: What are you trapped by?

DANIEL: Open space for one thing. I think I've come down with agoraphobia.

MORGAN: You don't come down with agrophobia; it's not the flu. I should have seen this coming a long time ago. You were always sensitive, always a little low-grade OCD.

DANIEL: I'm not OCD. I'm not OCD. I'm not OCD. I have to say that three times for some reason.

MORGAN: I don't think it's going to be a big deal. We can solve it.

DANIEL: Morgan, it's bad. I can't even open the blinds—the view, that expansive view that Mom loved so much, over the drop-off, into the valley, the sight of it fills me with terror. It's like I'm not in control of my own body. It shuts down.

MORGAN: Just so you know, we've only got a couple more minutes left.

DANIEL: When I look out there, it feels like it's pulling me, like I'll be vacuumed out through the glass and into nothingness.

MORGAN: It's double-paned. Very low risk.

DANIEL: And … did you see that pile of clothes on the floor?

MORGAN: Yeah.

DANIEL: I'm sleeping there now.

MORGAN: You sleep on a pile of clothes? Like a hamster?

DANIEL: Oh, nice work on building a safe environment, doctor.

MORGAN: No, it's just that I threw my undies in there. I thought it was a cold wash.

DANIEL: You brought laundry?

MORGAN: Well, I brought all my clothes.

DANIEL: Why? Oh no, you're not staying here.

MORGAN: You'd have trouble finding another therapist who's that committed.

DANIEL: No. Uh-uh. I can't live with another person.

MORGAN: It'll do you good.

DANIEL: No way. I'll find your hair in the tub. Just that alone … ·

MORGAN: My roommate kicked me out.

DANIEL: What? Why?

MORGAN: Why? He's a manipative psycho. And that is not a judgment. I am very understanding of mental disorders—I'm a therapist. But he was a very uptight man.

DANIEL: I'm uptight.

MORGAN: But in a lovable way. And the vacancy rate is like percent. I'm kind of stranded.

DANIEL: Well, I can help you look. I've got high-speed.

MORGAN: Hey, this isn't *your* house. I grew up here too, you know.

DANIEL: But I've been living here for a while, taking care of Mom.

MORGAN: And now I'm taking care of you. Daniel. Please.

DANIEL: Okay, just for a bit. But you have to wax your body hair.

MORGAN: Already do. And that's time … there. Let's get you to bed. Your real bed.

DANIEL: No. I just can't. I feel too … far off the ground.

MORGAN: Two feet?

DANIEL: It doesn't matter. It's the feeling of falling. Every night, every single night, I'm dreaming that I'm falling. Always falling. No matter how it starts, it always ends the same.

MORGAN: Tell me.

ANXIETY

*The scene shifts to a montage of physical images that reveal the
barrage of anxiety dreams that DANIEL faces nightly.*

DANIEL: I'm running. I'm late for a trigonometry exam, but as I run I realize: I haven't made it to a single class all year; I'm in my thirties at serious risk of failing grade twelve; and my high school seems to have been merged with a discount lingerie store whose layout is both confusing and arousing. And then I remember I have to complete the

Marathon of Hope for Terry Fox and I wonder, "How can I make it from Thunder Bay to Victoria in fifteen minutes?" But I decide to try.

So I pull out a can of Alphaghetti for energy—and to spell the word "hope" on my T-shirt so people will love me—but I don't have a can opener, so I attempt to bite my way into the can and all of my teeth begin to break off in the process. So I leave the marathon and head home to floss, hoping I can repair what's left with better periodontal care, but the floss is like piano wire and my gums are bleeding and more teeth are being taken out and then I realize I'm wearing my shoes from the marathon and I'm sure I've tracked in all sorts of fecal matter from the road and the floss has been dragging on the ground. Bleeding gums. Contamination. So I call 9-1-1 to get a Hepatitis A shot and some condoms to be delivered by the Panago Pizza guy, but I keep misdialling: 9-1-2, 9-1-4, 8-1-1, 9-Volume-Flash, and so on … Then I notice my phone is a pay phone and I need a quarter. I have a handful of change and it's all euros and chocolate coins from the White Spot, but I do find one quarter, which I drop under the bed. I reach under to grab it, and something bites me. I look, and there's a whole colony of rabbits living under my bed, tons of them. And so I grab the DustBuster hoping I can clear them out. I start by sucking up the little baby rabbits, and there's this horrible scream—the scream of dying rabbits. So I reverse the vacuum to spit the rabbits out, but the wind from the DustBuster starts to tear the place apart and the walls blow down and I'm on the edge of this outrageously tall building, fighting to hang on to what little structure remains in the middle of this hurricane, and then I slip and I fall …

DANIEL falls. The sound of roaring wind.

PARATHERAPY

DANIEL returns to the living room to face MORGAN.

MORGAN: I may have a solution. But it's radical.

DANIEL: What?

MORGAN: Paratherapy.

DANIEL: "Paratherapy"?

MORGAN: It's something I'm pioneering: a combination of traditional counselling mixed with a physical regimen.

DANIEL: How physical?

MORGAN: Extreme sports.

DANIEL: How extreme?

MORGAN: Skydiving.

DANIEL: Skydiving?

MORGAN: Skydiving. It's—

He holds his hands up, palms together.

MORGAN: —you (*one hand*). Your fear (*the other hand*).

He slaps his hands together.

MORGAN: Face on. It's a deep tissue massage for your soul. Release those psychic cramps and spiritual kinks.

DANIEL: You're serious?

MORGAN: You have to do something; you're dying here.

DANIEL: But, Morgan, really—skydiving? Currently I can't use a public toilet.

MORGAN: That's okay, you can go before.

DANIEL: No, I'm saying I can't get out of the house; I'm agoraphobic. And I don't think a person can experience much more "agora" than jumping from ten thousand feet in the air.

MORGAN: I'd like to suggest thirteen to fifteen thousand feet—for the extra free-fall time.

DANIEL: You're not much of a therapist; you know that, don't you?

MORGAN: What?

DANIEL: Isn't there some sort of code, some sort of Hippocratic Oath, in which you swear not to endanger a patient's life?

MORGAN: Not that I'm aware of. But I do know that my brand of therapy doesn't fart around spinning its wheels navel-gazing; it just cuts straight to the core issue.

DANIEL: Which is?

MORGAN: Which is ... fear ... of ... falling ... for one ... and ... uh, I don't know, maybe something about Mom?

DANIEL: You don't have a clue.

MORGAN: I have more than a clue. I have an answer. "Paratherapy."

DANIEL: *Para*therapy? Hmm ... Let's just run that through the bullshit meter.

> *DANIEL mimes a handheld device and makes an alarm sound as he passes it over MORGAN.*

MORGAN: Oh yeah? "Para" means beyond. So therapy through skydiving is paratherapy because you're pushing "beyond" your fears and you're wearing a parachute. It works on multiple levels.

DANIEL: Except you don't know what you're talking about. You've never even skydived.

MORGAN: Oh, haven't I?

DANIEL: You have?

MORGAN: Impressed?

DANIEL: Surprised.

MORGAN: I joined a club.

DANIEL: I can't believe it.

MORGAN: It's amazing, Daniel; you have to try it.

DANIEL: No, I certainly do not.

MORGAN: You do. It was on our list.

DANIEL: What list?

MORGAN: Of things to do when we grew up.

DANIEL: Oh.

MORGAN: It was a pact.

DANIEL: We were kids.

MORGAN: A pact. We signed it. In blood.

DANIEL: Blood. You're dreaming.

MORGAN: How did you get that scar on your hand?

DANIEL: I've always had it.

Shows his palm.

MORGAN: Me too.

DANIEL: Birthmark.

MORGAN: Well, we're not identical twins. We don't have the same birthmarks.

DANIEL: And so you did it, fulfilled your destiny.

MORGAN: No, the destiny was us doing it together. And you know I'm right. This is something deeper than just a stunt; it's at the core of your being—the heart of your desires.

DANIEL turns away.

MORGAN: Hmm? What did you say?

DANIEL: I didn't say anything. I was just thinking.

MORGAN: About what?

DANIEL: About whether or not I've ever heard a stupider idea.

MORGAN: It'll work!

DANIEL: Even if it did work … just think about it for a second, Morgan. How am I supposed to even get to the airplane?

MORGAN: Training. Paratherapy is a rigorous discipline. We have to work your mind, your spirit, and your body. I'll be your personal trainer.

DANIEL: You? Mr. Beer Belly?

MORGAN: I have core strength. And I have I have my pie-lats certificate.

DANIEL: You don't have a pilot's license. You have a pilot's licence?

MORGAN: No, not a pilot's licence, pielats … or pie-lates.

DANIEL: What are you saying?

MORGAN: It's an exercise technique—tones, increases flexibility, builds core strength …

DANIEL: Do you mean Pilates?

MORGAN: No … pie-lates.

DANIEL: It's Pilates, you idiot.

MORGAN: Is it?

DANIEL: How are you supposed to teach it; you can't even say it.

MORGAN: Well, I'm not teaching pronounciation.

DANIEL: "Pro*nun*ciation."

MORGAN: Huh? Really?

DANIEL: Yes.

MORGAN: Shit. I've been pro-nun-cing it wrong all these years.

DANIEL: Holy Chaka Khan, Morgan; are you deliberately trying to give me a seizure?

MORGAN: It'll be a logical series of steps. Like a prize-fighter working out! Remember Survivor? "Eye of the Tiger"? Come on:

MORGAN sings the open bass riff to Survivor's "Eye of the Tiger" and starts throwing punches.

MORGAN: Dow! Da-da Dow Dow Dow, Da-da Dow Dow Dow, Da-da Dow Dow Downnn. Pick it up!

DANIEL reluctantly joins in on the bass line to "Eye of the Tiger." MORGAN sings to the rhythm of the opening riff.

MORGAN: "We'll get you up off the floor / Back into bed / Nighty-night." "Open the blinds / look at the birds / see them fly"—Then: "Climb up a ladder / stand on the roof / swing your hips."

DANIEL: Hips?

MORGAN: Yeah, rock it! "Catch a bus / go to the mall / buy some pants." Here we go (*breaks into full melody*): "Book a seat / fly through the sky / jump from a plane like an eagle!"

DANIEL: Hold it. You went from buying pants to jumping out of a plane?

MORGAN: When you look good, you feel good.

DANIEL: No, Morgan, I'm not going to do that.

MORGAN: Don't you want your life back?

DANIEL: I'll just maybe work on my breathing exercises.

MORGAN: Give me sixty seconds to change your mind.

DANIEL: Sixty seconds?

MORGAN: That's the time of a free-fall.

DANIEL: I could never do it.

MORGAN: Well, here's why you might. A little secret: when you free-fall, you don't feel the fall, only the free. At terminal velocity there's no more acceleration and the feeling of falling just evaporates off your skin. And what you actually feel is that you're sitting on this tremendous tower of wind blowing up from some giant mouth below. Like you're floating on the exhalation of God. And with the smallest movements of your body, you direct rushing wind to take you wherever you want to go. Move your hand like this, and you're spinning ecstatically; arch your back and lift your chin, and you flip. You can soar, glide, swoop, dive, and tumble. And for sixty seconds, there's no more up or down, no gravity holding you, no objects, buildings, or land to define yourself against. You are above the world, which is now only an idea. And for a moment you understand that you are only your body—its sensations, memories, and dreams.

Your physical being defines all space and time with nothing else to overshadow you. Daniel, you fly. Not only in the air, but in your soul. And with this freedom, you know what it is to be alive because you've seen the bigger world inside you.

Music. The men briefly soar.

TRUST

There's a shift and DANIEL has his back to MORGAN. They're practising trust exercises. MORGAN holds his hands out a couple of inches from DANIEL, and DANIEL falls back into his hands.

MORGAN: Beautiful. You're doing great, Daniel. Keep your eyes closed. Try it again.

MORGAN lets him fall a little farther.

MORGAN: Gorgeous. Well done. Drop your shoulders. Relax. Again.

MORGAN lets him go a little farther again.

MORGAN: Woah, nice.

DANIEL: That's good for now. I'm feeling a little shaky.

MORGAN: One more.

DANIEL: No farther though.

MORGAN: A little farther.

DANIEL: No, the same. Or not at all.

MORGAN: Oh, all right. The same. Relax. Breathe. Shoulders. Good. And go.

DANIEL falls back; MORGAN pulls his hands away and DANIEL falls. Suddenly he's tumbling through space desperately clawing at his parachute trying to find the cord. Shift.

THE LUCIDITY INSTITUTE

DANIEL lies in bed holding an ice pack to his head.

MORGAN: Shit, Danny, I'm sorry. I didn't think you'd hit the coffee table. You're longer than you seem.

DANIEL: What were you thinking?

MORGAN: I just wanted you to break through the fear. You know? Feel the falling sensation and then when you hit the ground you know that there's nothing to worry about; it doesn't hurt. That's why I had the foamy there. Stupid coffee table.

DANIEL: Stupid coffee table? I'll show you stupid.

MORGAN: We'll try it again, when you're feeling better.

DANIEL: No way. No more trust exercises.

MORGAN: Why not?

DANIEL: Because I don't trust you.

MORGAN: You said that with great confidence, which means you trust yourself. So I'm going to mark that as a success. And besides, look at you. You're back in your bed! Double-victory.

DANIEL: And a possible concussion.

MORGAN: Just keep that on your head. You know what? When I went for the ice pack, I made a startling discovery.

DANIEL: What?

MORGAN: Mom has birds in the freezer.

DANIEL: Oh yeah.

MORGAN: I don't mean chicken. There are a bunch of dead birds— finches, robins, jays, a gull—wrapped in paper towel and frozen.

DANIEL: I know.

MORGAN: You know? What's that about? It's creepy as hell.

DANIEL: Welcome to Mom's secret world. As far as I've been able to glean, birds would fly into that picture window and, you know, crunch, and she felt bad I guess, or something. Responsible. So she would pick them up and if they didn't survive, they'd go in the freezer.

MORGAN: Why didn't she just put them in the garbage?

DANIEL: Maybe respect? I think she wanted to bury them, but could never get around to it. So ... bird morgue.

MORGAN: Intense.

DANIEL: There's something even more intense down there.

MORGAN: What's that?

DANIEL: I'll show you.

> *DANIEL guides MORGAN to the basement.*

DANIEL: Look.

MORGAN: Woah. What is it?

DANIEL: I call it "the Archives."

MORGAN: Does she not throw anything out? It's floor to ceiling boxes.

DANIEL: Most of that is ours you know. Stuff from when we were kids.

MORGAN: Oh? I should go and dig out my old Hawk Rider outfit!

DANIEL: I doubt your Hawk Rider outfit would still fit.

MORGAN: You can always fit in spandex.

> *Shift. DANIEL turns and talks to us.*

DANIEL: In the late 1980s, Morgan formed a garage band called Hawk Rider. In art class he commissioned the most talented airbrush artist to come up with a series of album covers that would always feature a giant hawk and a large-breasted woman in a chainmail bikini. He had it all planned out: the entire arc of the band.

The debut album would feature the soaring hawk in the night sky, with the girl riding it wearing an expression of orgasmic ecstasy. The hawk held a guitar in its talons and the album was called *Rock-Turnal Hunter*. Then the sophomore follow-up album was called *Hawk Hard* and featured the same hawk portrayed as a marble statue atop a gravestone, with the nearly naked girl weeping at its feet.

The third album, and my absolute favourite design of all, was to be called *Birds of Prey* and featured the girl, now entirely naked, except for a falcon's hood, perched impossibly on the hawk's "wrist," as if about to take off. How did the artist make that hawk look so horny? Unfortunately Morgan always skipped band practice to work on the promo-materials for albums and songs that didn't exist. So they never recorded an album or even wrote any original material, and eventually ended up just playing Top 40 covers.

Restore.

MORGAN: What's so funny?

DANIEL: Nothing … something unrelated flashed into my head.

MORGAN: Do you think the pact is here?

MORGAN is scanning the boxes.

DANIEL: Maybe. We should sort through it all though. Purge and clean out the basement.

MORGAN: Why? This is gold mine!

DANIEL: Well, Mom's not going to be well enough to live here again. We'll probably have to sell the place eventually.

MORGAN: But we live here.

DANIEL: No, *I* live here; you're visiting.

MORGAN: You can't sell it if you can't leave it.

DANIEL: I know; that's why I've got to beat this thing.

MORGAN has locked onto a specific box.

MORGAN: Patience, Daniel-San. One step at a time. I've just found the next phase of paratherapy for you here.

DANIEL: What is it, Mr. Miyagi?

MORGAN: Miya-*gi*! Miya-*gi*! Self-help instructional videos. I forgot all about these.

DANIEL reads the box covers.

DANIEL: *Falling in Love with Yourself: Inner Seduction Techniques, Men's Drumming Circle: Part One, The Loin Kings?*—oh my lord, Morgan—*The Art of Lucid Dreaming.*

MORGAN: That's the one!

DANIEL: This is all old new age bullshit. I don't want to watch—Hey. Don't put that in; I just cleaned the heads on that.

MORGAN: Watch! Listen! Learn!

MORGAN plugs the video in. New age music plays.

DANIEL: Nice graphics. When was this made? 1988?

MORGAN: (*checks the box*) Uh … no '85.

A cheesy voice is heard from the TV.

HOST: Oh, hello. I did see you come in. I felt your presence by expanding the energy receptors of my mind.

Welcome to part VII in the Doors of Perception series of instructional videos. Today's episode: *Lucid Dreaming.*

Music. MORGAN's voice begins to overlap with the recording until he becomes the host of the program on the TV.

HOST: Lucid dreaming is a technique that has been practised by shamans, vision seekers, and prophets through the ages.

DANIEL shakes his head skeptically.

MORGAN: (*as host*) A lucid dream is a dream in which you are aware that you're in a dream and, being so, have control over both your actions and your environment.

DANIEL: Is this real?

MORGAN: You can see, hear, taste, smell, and feel as if in a waking state, but have the power to do supernatural things.

DANIEL: Supernatural?

MORGAN: Be invisible, walk through walls, lift a locomotive above your head, travel to the Moon, go back in time, or make love to whomever, however you please.

DANIEL: Cool.

MORGAN winks at DANIEL.

MORGAN: Suffer from phobias?

DANIEL: Yes, I do.

MORGAN: You can battle and conquer them in your dreams. '

DANIEL: Dreams.

MORGAN: Dreams. Solve problems, recover memories, revisit traumatic experiences, and defeat the demons that haunt you, all while asleep.

DANIEL: Wow.

MORGAN: Wow, people say …

TOGETHER: But how?

MORGAN: Well, with simple techniques, you first learn to become aware of your dream life, then to become conscious within it, then to hold on to it instead of waking without control. When you've mastered that, you will be the architect of all that you desire.

The HOST's voice returns and MORGAN's fades out.

DANIEL: Yes!

HOST: And then you will do what humans have longed to do since the dawn time—perform that impossible action, that action which represents ultimate freedom and escape from life's physical, emotional, and psychological restraints:

ALL: You will fly!

The video gets snapped off. MORGAN raises his eyebrows to DANIEL.

MORGAN: Eh?

DANIEL: Yeah.

MORGAN: Eh?

DANIEL: Yeah.

MORGAN: Eh?

DANIEL: Oh yeah!

MORGAN rocks out with his air guitar, and DANIEL picks up an airbass; they go back to back and rock out together in silence. After a couple of bars:

DANIEL: What are you playing?

MORGAN: Ozzy! What are you playing?

DANIEL: (*embarrassed*) Um … Parachute Club.

MORGAN: Parachute Club?

Pause.

MORGAN: Nice! CanCon!

Music blasts and they rock out some more, floating into a new position.

NOSTALGIA

In the Archives. The men are playing a game of Pong. Their bodies are the paddles.

MORGAN: Ah, the good old Atari.

DANIEL: Pong hasn't aged very well.

MORGAN: Great for the reflexes. Part of the training.

DANIEL: Can you at least make an effort to disguise the fact that you're pulling this therapy out of your ass.

MORGAN: You know who was good at Pong? What's-her-name. From the debate club.

DANIEL: Oh yeah, uh, what's-her-face.

MORGAN: No, no, not what's-her-face, but the other one. You know, um, what's-her-name.

DANIEL: You're talking about the one that had the improperly sized glass eye that made it seem like she was always looking through a magnifying glass and about to exclaim something like, "I say!"

MORGAN: No, the other one.

DANIEL: Who then? Oh, her. Oh, yeah, yeah, the one that pulled the Tonya Harding on the grass hockey captain.

MORGAN: No. She was completely exhumed from those charges.

DANIEL: You mean exonerated.

MORGAN: Potato, po-tah-to.

DANIEL: Um ... that's more like potato, potassium.

MORGAN: I think potatoes are mostly starch.

DANIEL: I'm going to kill myself.

DANIEL wins the Pong game.

MORGAN: (*as William Shatner in* Star Trek II) Khan!

Beat.

MORGAN: I wish I could remember her name. I'd like to google her. Track her down.

The men start to drift together into a casual sitting position.

DANIEL: Why do you want to track her down?

MORGAN: Nostalgia. She was something else. Maybe she would be nostalgic too—you know, the classic "one for old time's sake."

DANIEL: Oh, Morgan. The human body regenerates every seven years, you know. All new material. Whoever you remember is long gone. She's had two entirely different bodies since you saw her last.

MORGAN: But not the brain. Its cells don't get replaced. That part's permanent. And they say it's the most important sex organ.

DANIEL: You don't believe that.

MORGAN: You're right; I totally prefer my penis. Bingo. That's what we need to do: we need to hook you up with a lady. For therapeutic purposes.

DANIEL: No thanks.

MORGAN: Oh, come on. When was the last time you—

DANIEL: Morgan. I said no.

MORGAN: I am opening my little black book to a page at random: "Jenny." Who the hell is Jenny? Oh well, start somewhere. Take this down: 604—

DANIEL: I met someone online.

Beat.

MORGAN: Oh. I did not know this. And?

DANIEL: And, well I ended up on a date.

MORGAN: Oh, really? Good for you. When?

DANIEL: A while back—when I could still get outside now and then.

MORGAN: So what was she like?

DANIEL: She was seven-foot-one.

MORGAN: That's quite tall.

DANIEL: Oh, is that what that is? Morgan, seven-foot-one; she was taller than Master-Blaster in *Mad Max Beyond Thunderdome*.

Pause.

MORGAN: Are you including the midget that sat on Master-Blaster's shoulders?

DANIEL: Of course I'm including the midget! The name "Master-Blaster" automatically includes the midget! The midget was "Master" and the big baby-faced wrestler guy he rode was "Blaster"! That was the genius of the whole character, for chrissakes! They were two outcasts that together made a single powerful and VERY TALL entity. And that was the original point of my reference: my date was as tall—or taller than— a very large wrestler wearing a midget stacked on top. And explaining it has totally robbed the value of the allusion.

MORGAN: You know what your superpower is?

DANIEL: What?

MORGAN: Indignant rage. When placed in an emotionally vulnerable position, you can fly into a tizzy over the most meaningless thing. It's a means of creating a smokescreen—like ink from the ass of a giant squid.

Beat.

MORGAN: So?

DANIEL: So.

MORGAN: Was she nice?

DANIEL: Sure.

MORGAN: What does she do?

DANIEL: Kindergarten teacher.

MORGAN: Oh yeah?

DANIEL: Her students come up to the middle of her shin.

MORGAN: So, was the date a dud?

DANIEL: What do you think?

MORGAN: Was she personable?

DANIEL: Very.

MORGAN: Interesting?

DANIEL: Very. She speaks four languages, co-owns a racehorse named Ever Since the Events of 9/11, has a step-brother who she rescued from the Scientologists, plays the, you know, crystal glasses full of water, really well.

MORGAN: That sounds like your checklist. Was she attractive?

DANIEL: I guess that's the problem.

MORGAN: Couldn't get over the height?

DANIEL: I found it incredibly arousing.

MORGAN: Continue.

DANIEL: Throughout the date, I became obsessed. And she was terribly attractive and totally unassuming—you know, no pretensions. I instantly knew that people didn't notice how gorgeous she was because she was so freakishly large. And I was excited that I discovered a hidden secret. But then I just began to fixate on her looks. Every part of her was perfect, but simply super-sized. And that drove me even more crazy. I wanted her to pick me up and cup me in her hands. I wanted to just crawl inside her.

MORGAN: For her to unbirth you.

DANIEL: What?

MORGAN: To crawl back to the womb. That's normal.

43

DANIEL: A: That's not what I meant. And 2: That's not normal.

MORGAN: A: It's exactly what you said. And 2: Whatever turns you on. Did you sleep with her?

DANIEL: No. The point is it became too much to bear. I didn't want to develop some fetish. And it wasn't about crawling in the womb. I just wanted her to ... smother me.

Pause.

MORGAN: I was nearly smothered by a woman. It was terrifying.

DANIEL: What?

MORGAN: One night a neighbour came by—she lived across the hall in the other place, and she was really nice. She'd come over sometimes and help with stuff now and then. Talk in the elevator. Stuff like that. Well, she shows up and tells me she's moving to Brandon. Fiancé's got a job there with the provincial department of highways. So she's moving. And she wanted to say goodbye and have sex.

DANIEL: Hold it. What-what-what-what ... What?

MORGAN: She'd had this crush apparently and decided it was now or never.

DANIEL: She was engaged.

MORGAN: I wasn't gonna tell him.

DANIEL: But—

MORGAN: This happens more often than you think.

DANIEL: To you or in general?

MORGAN: Both.

DANIEL: My neighbours never come over and ask for sex.

MORGAN shrugs.

DANIEL: So how did she smother you? Did she turn out to be a psycho?

MORGAN: No. She was sitting on my face and she formed a perfect seal over my mouth and nose.

DANIEL: What? You couldn't get out?

MORGAN: Oh yeah, she was right into it. Right at the edge, you know. Nothing was going to get her off until she got off. I mean I was pushing, thrashing, hitting at her, but it only made her more excited.

DANIEL: What did you do?

MORGAN: The only thing I could. As my life flashed before my eyes, survival instinct kicked in. I thought, "Lick fast or die."

DANIEL: So did she get off?

MORGAN: Yes and yes.

DANIEL: And what did you say?

In answer to the question, MORGAN inhales like he's just come up from 20,000 leagues under the sea.

DANIEL: Wow. I can't believe the bullshit you come up with.

MORGAN: What?

DANIEL: Do you think that's actually true—that when you die your life flashes before your eyes?

MORGAN: I know it's true. It goes in reverse. What's really wild was realizing that if I didn't get out of there, the last thing I would ever see would have also been the very first thing I ever saw.

MORGAN nods suggestively.

MORGAN: But it would have been the way to go for sure.

DANIEL: I don't buy it.

MORGAN: The life before your eyes?

DANIEL: Yeah.

MORGAN: I guess you have to experience it for yourself. It's the detail that's extraordinary.

>*Shift.*

PRELUDE TO A NIGHTMARE

Wind. DANIEL is falling helplessly until: splash. The environment transforms and he now floats through a weird underwater environment. There is a repeated, echoing "ping" sound that might be a submarine's sonar or it might be the sound of a heart monitor in a hospital. DANIEL swims beneath the surface in the murky green-blue that grows darker as he dives farther down. He has an underwater light and is searching for something as he dives deeper and deeper. He catches something in the light. Standing on the ocean floor, holding his breath, is MORGAN. DANIEL grabs his hand and tries to pull him to the surface, but he won't move. MORGAN shakes his head helplessly and points down. DANIEL swims lower and digs with his hands around MORGAN's feet. Something is holding him down.

Running out of oxygen, DANIEL is scrambling to free his brother. He can't do it. He starts to drift upwards and MORGAN is swallowed by blackness.

BIONICS

Shift. Pre-dawn. Inside the Archives. DANIEL is hyperventilating as MORGAN enters.

MORGAN: What are you doing?

DANIEL: Couldn't sleep.

MORGAN: Nightmares?

DANIEL: I dreamt that I thought I could fly.

MORGAN: That's great!

DANIEL: Except when I tried to get off the ground I couldn't totally do it. My head seemed to be extraordinarily heavy, and it sort of dragged on the ground, bumping along. Humiliating. And you were ...

MORGAN: I was ...?

DANIEL: Nothing. I can't remember.

MORGAN: Lucid dreaming doesn't happen overnight. Well, I guess it does eventually, but ... Have you been keeping up with the techniques?

DANIEL: Yeah.

MORGAN: "Am I dreaming?"

DANIEL: Yes, I'm doing them.

MORGAN: Good. "Am I dreaming?" You've got to make that question really present in your conscious mind so that it will start to show up in your dream life. "Am I ..."

DANIEL: Yeah. Anyway, thought I'd just keep cleaning out down here.

MORGAN starts rummaging through the boxes with DANIEL.

MORGAN: Oh, look at this great stuff: *Dukes of Hazzard* Thermos, *Breakfast Club* soundtrack with a heart drawn around Molly Ringwald ...

DANIEL: Hey!

DANIEL pulls out an action figure from the mix.

MORGAN: Six Million Dollar Man!

TOGETHER: "Steve Austin, astronaut, a man barely alive. Gentlemen, we can rebuild him, we have the technology. We have the capability to make the world's first bionic man. Steve Austin will be that man. Better than he was before. Better. Stronger. Faster."

MORGAN sings the theme song. DANIEL looks through the back of the doll's head.

DANIEL: I'll use my bionic eye to spy on Lindsay Wagner in the shower.

MORGAN: Bionic sex.

DANIEL: This is best feature: when you look through the bionic eye on this doll everything just seems farther away and out of focus.

MORGAN: Here let me see.

MORGAN reaches for it, but DANIEL makes Steve jump out of the way using his bionic powers.

DANIEL: Nope. I'm still looking at it.

MORGAN: Give it; that was mine.

DANIEL: No, it wasn't.

MORGAN: Yeah.

DANIEL: No! I had Steve Austin, and you had Stretch Armstrong.

MORGAN: No, I—Oh, yeah. Stretch. That thing was hideous. Where is he, I wonder?

DANIEL: Garbage.

MORGAN: No!

DANIEL: Well, you wrecked it—you cut him open to see what made him stretchy.

MORGAN: I did?

DANIEL: Yeah, remember? It was full of dense purple goo and you told me it was the same filling that was in a Big Turk.

MORGAN: I don't remember this.

DANIEL: Sure you do. I was rushed to the hospital because of it, moron. Mom called poison control and said, "My son's eaten the filling out of a Stretch Armstrong doll! What do I do?" It wasn't on their list. "Sorry, ma'am, we've got Spray 'n Wash, then Static Guard, but no Stretch Armstrong." I had my freakin' stomach pumped.

MORGAN: Maybe that's the beginning of all your obsessions.

DANIEL: If anything, it should have made me fear my idiot big brother and his continuous plots to kill me.

MORGAN takes the Steve Austin figure.

MORGAN: We will rebuild you. Better than you were before. Hook you up with the Bionic Woman.

DANIEL: Jaime Sommers.

MORGAN: How did the Bionic Woman become bionic anyway?

DANIEL: On a date with Steve Austin.

MORGAN: Really?

DANIEL: They went skydiving together. Her chute malfunctioned. Steve used his pull at the OSI to get her bionic limbs.

MORGAN: Cyber-romance.

DANIEL: Except ... her head injury erased her memory. She no longer knew she loved Colonel Austin.

MORGAN: How ironic.

DANIEL: How many people die each year from skydiving?

MORGAN: Ask, rather, how many survive?

DANIEL: How many?

MORGAN: Most.

DANIEL: Most.

Pause.

MORGAN: "Am I dreaming?"

DANIEL: "Am I dreaming?"

MORGAN: Answer.

DANIEL: "No, I'm not dreaming."

MORGAN: How do you know?

DANIEL: I know I'm awake because … well, it just feels normal. I'm aware, and I'm aware that I'm aware. I can't change my environment. And things remain stable: I look at my watch, look away and look back, and it says the same time and I can read the word "Casio," which is very tiny print—all of which they say you can't do in a dream.

MORGAN: Good stuff. Small text is very unstable in a dream. I'm checking my watch all the time now.

DANIEL: Where did you get that? Is that new?

MORGAN: No, man, it's my old Swatch that I got at the Swiss Pavilion at Expo. I thought I'd lost it.

DANIEL: It's so big. And colourful.

MORGAN: That was the style. "Swatch."

DANIEL: Wait, what time is it?

MORGAN: Five-fifteen.

DANIEL: Sunrise soon. Mom's favourite time of day. She's got to be lonely, eh?

MORGAN: Don't beat yourself up.

DANIEL: Why don't you go visit her?

MORGAN: I don't really want to see her like this. She probably won't
know who I am. I might freak her out. "Stranger!" I don't want that. It's
just so depressing. I want to remember Mom like she was.

DANIEL: But Mom *is*. You know? She's not past tense. You owe her a visit.

MORGAN: You just worry about what *you* owe.

DANIEL: Well, I owe her a visit too.

MORGAN: Well keep working at the dreaming then. Hey! Look.

*MORGAN pulls out a little plastic paratrooper figure with a tiny
parachute attached.*

MORGAN: Remember?

DANIEL: Oh yeah, those guys.

MORGAN: We used to throw these off the roof and see if we could get
them sailing down over the edge and into the valley.

DANIEL: Oh yeah. We were grounded for being on the roof.

MORGAN: No one to say anything now. I know you wanna.

DANIEL: I don't know … the roof?

MORGAN: How about that big, scary living room window? Come on!

Music. The men charge out and up to the window.

TOYS FROM HEAVEN

The men are leaning out the window, poised to throw the parachute men.

MORGAN: Come on! You can do it; chuck it over!

DANIEL: Okay, okay. Just a second.

MORGAN: Chuck it!

DANIEL: Oh my god, we're in our thirties.

MORGAN: Chuck it!

DANIEL: Okay, okay!

DANIEL drops the parachute guy over the edge.

DANIEL: Look out below!

MORGAN: Incoming.

DANIEL: I hope some kid finds those.

MORGAN: Toys from Heaven.

DANIEL: I'm getting some déjà vu. Like when we were little.

MORGAN: You're doing great, Dan. I'm really impressed.

DANIEL: Oh, crap. I think I have to close the window. I'm feeling the vertigo.

MORGAN: All right. But we'll keep the blinds open. Enjoy the view. And breathe. Good.

DANIEL: Yeah, not so bad.

MORGAN: Exactly. You're safe. You're here. I'm here. Wouldn't want to be anywhere else. And look at that view! Sunrise. Clouds on fire. Majestic eagle soaring over the valley.

DANIEL: That's a seagull.

MORGAN: Oh yeah … but he's a beaut'. Salut, my wingéd brother. See that flying, what ease, what grace …

DANIEL: What is he doing?

TOGETHER: Shit!

Bang! The sound of bird hitting glass. The guys watch as the bird slides down the pane into a sticky mess below.

MORGAN: Blinds shut?

DANIEL: Blinds shut.

Shift.

SWAN SONG

Sound of gentle breeze. Some crickets.

DANIEL: It's chilly. Let's get started.

MORGAN: Dearly beloved, we are gathered to say farewell to our fine feathered friend and all of his frozen brothers who have come before, like Icarus, pursuing their dreams, but in their ambition flying too close to the sun—except in this case, the house.

DANIEL: Well, let's just bury them and get inside.

MORGAN: Buried!

DANIEL: What?

MORGAN: I just remembered what happened to the skydiving pact.

DANIEL: What?

MORGAN: We buried it. At the old campsite. In a time capsule.

DANIEL: Time capsule. I totally forgot about that. We did bury a time capsule. What was in it?

MORGAN: The pact. And I think some Pop Rocks and a can of Coke. Oh, Danny, we should go dig it up.

DANIEL: That was like twenty-five years ago.

MORGAN: That's exactly the point of a time capsule. Wouldn't it be fantastic? There might be other little treasures there as well. Let's do it.

DANIEL: But my agoraphobia.

MORGAN: Dude! Look at you. You're outside. It's a victory, man.

DANIEL: True. But I don't know that I can actually go as far as camping.

MORGAN: I think you can. And further.

DANIEL: But why does everything have to be what you want? You know, it's always your idea of what we should do.

MORGAN: Well, what do you want to do?

DANIEL: I want to finish this funeral and go back inside. I'm exhausted.

MORGAN: Fine. But don't throw the dirt on yet. I brought the old boom-box out for funeral music.

DANIEL: What funeral music do you have?

MORGAN: Flock of Seagulls. This one's for you, J. Livingston.

Music. Shift as the men float skyward.

R.E.M.

DANIEL and MORGAN lie side by side in their beds from childhood.

DANIEL: "Am I dreaming?"

MORGAN: "Am I dreaming?"

DANIEL: "Am I dreaming?"

MORGAN: Okay now; put these on.

DANIEL puts on a pair of god-awful sunglasses.

DANIEL: What do they do?

MORGAN: They're Lucid Dreaming Glasses. But I want to rename them. What do you like: "Dream Shades"? "Moon-Glasses"? Get some ad time on late-night cable.

DANIEL: What do they do?

MORGAN: They detect when you're entering R.E.M. sleep—essentially the point right at the beginning of the dream state. And then there are these little LEDs in the frame that start to flash and show up in your dream environment letting you know that you're dreaming.

DANIEL: How are you supposed to sleep wearing flashing glasses?

MORGAN: How did the first Eskimo sleep in an igloo? "I can't sleep here; this is a house made of ice." But he gave it a try and ... "Hmm, not so bad. Kinda cozy." You can get used to anything.

DANIEL: Flashing lights?

MORGAN: Northern Lights?

Dumbfounded beat.

MORGAN: They don't flash until you're sleeping, so they're not keeping you awake. And what happens is you come to recognize these flashing lights as a cue inside your dream that lets you know you're dreaming. The moment of lucidity. At that point you can take control.

DANIEL: Where did you get these?

MORGAN: I invented them.

DANIEL: You invented them?

MORGAN: Well, I got them on the internet.

DANIEL: That's not the same.

MORGAN: I got the components on the internet and I modified them to suit my purposes.

DANIEL: How did you modify them?

MORGAN: Well, I painted them blue and put the sparkles on.

DANIEL: Did you get a patent on that, 'cause somewhere there's a girl in grade two who's totally infringing on your technology.

MORGAN: And I had to assemble them when they arrived. Put those arms on with the mini-screwdriver.

DANIEL: How exactly do they detect that I'm dreaming.

MORGAN: R.E.M. Rapid—or is it Random?—Eye. Movement. It detects the motion of your eyes.

DANIEL: Yes, but how?

MORGAN: It has these little infrared motion detectors in the centre of each lens.

DANIEL: So it's shooting my eyes with infrared radiation?

MORGAN: It's not dangerous.

DANIEL: How do you know?

MORGAN: It's the same technology that's in your TV's remote control—you're not afraid to use that are you?

DANIEL: Well, I don't shoot it point-blank into my eyeball for eight consecutive hours.

MORGAN: You could. It would be safe. Just try them. They're bound to work.

Shift.

SIREN'S CALL

Night. Crickets. Loud hum of a refrigerator.

DANIEL: I can't sleep. Stupid glasses digging into my face. Morgan snores like he did when we were kids—the phlegmy gurgle of my youth. I walk around, talking to myself, narrating my environment, with the only light being from the neon sign flashing all film-noir style through the blinds. I look down, count the cars that pass the place—zero. It's dead out there. That horrible time between three and four when everyone's asleep and morning is so far away. I find myself at the front door holding the doorknob, turning it back and forth—rocking it back and forth like a cradle. My heart pounding like ... like ... like I have to—and suddenly, without warning, the door is open and I'm gone.

DANIEL puts on the shades. Music.

DANIEL: And I walk. I walk and I feel like I'm going the wrong way, making the wrong choice, crossing the tracks into the wrong part of town.

Everything's dark and shadowy—could be the sunglasses, but I don't want to be seen out here. I want to be anonymous—be someone else. And then, there: down at the end of the street, a red light glows in a window. My body threatening to shut right down with the overwhelming conflict of apprehension and desire. I get closer and I see the sheets of silk seductively draped behind the glass. The sensuous colours, the lipstick reds, the virginal whites, the delicate textures beckoning.

And behind them the straps, the cords, the clasps, clips, buckles, harnesses—medieval modern; high-tech sadistic. That red light blinking in the shape of a sign that reads: "Learn to Skydive." Oh god, I want it so bad.

Lights flash. Siren. Cops.

DANIEL: Shit. Cops.

VOICE: Hands behind your head.

DANIEL complies.

VOICE: Now cross them over your chest ...

DANIEL: (*confused*) Ooookay.

VOICE: Move them to your hips.

DANIEL: Hips?

VOICE: Are you questioning the Macarena?

DANIEL: No, ma'am. I'm just questioning why I'm doing it right now.

VOICE: Because I said so. Don't you know what flashing blue and red lights mean?

DANIEL: That you're a cop ...

VOICE: Damn straight.

DANIEL: ... or ... or ... that ... I'm ... a ...

Music.

"DREAMER"

A dream. A light picks out DANIEL strolling blissfully in a mysterious environment. He then walks along the stage floor. His steps get lighter and with each one he floats a little like he's walking on the Moon. He approaches the proscenium arch and walks up the side of it. He does a back-flip and begins to fly. His technique is a little awkward as he dog-paddles with his hands and does a sort of frog-legged kick with his feet.

The kindergarten teacher's dress descends from above. It sways seductively. He begins to swim towards it. He swims under it and then swims up inside the dress like a spawning salmon heading home. When he's almost completely concealed in the dress, it disappears and he's floating blissfully on his back.

From the grid fall many tiny parachutes. They float around him like jellyfish.

FLIGHT

DANIEL: It was fantastic, Morgan! I got in. I flew. I've never felt anything like it.

MORGAN: I knew it! You'll be flying for real in no time.

DANIEL: I feel so much more in control.

MORGAN: High five.

DANIEL: I want to go out.

MORGAN: Great!

DANIEL: I want to go—I want you and me to go and drop in on Mom. High five!

MORGAN: Oh. Uh ... yeah. Right, right. Maybe at some point.

DANIEL: No, tonight.

MORGAN: Tonight?

DANIEL: Why not?

MORGAN: Ah shoot, I've got something planned.

DANIEL: What?

MORGAN: Hawk Rider booked a gig.

DANIEL: Hawk Rider?

MORGAN: Yeah. Reunion concert. Bummer. Bad timing.

DANIEL: *Bummer?* This is huge, Morgan. I'm ready to do something here and I need your help.

MORGAN: I'm helping you by not going.

DANIEL: How?

MORGAN: It's a breakthrough. And it's better if I'm not holding your hand. You're on the edge now, so close to success. Time to leap in feet first. Just hold on to the feeling inside your dream. You're soaring, up, up, up ...

A BAR

The scene shifts to a bar. A classic '80s rock song—perhaps something like "Jump" by Van Halen—plays. MORGAN sings the song, but after a short time, he grows uncomfortable. Clearly the crowd isn't with him. His voice cracks.

The scene shifts to Mom's house.

PHONE CALL

DANIEL is at home, on the phone to MOM.

DANIEL: It's been a long time since I've felt this free. It's a fascinating technique. Maybe a little addictive too. But it's working. I dreamt I could come and visit, catch a bus, come to the hospital, and see you. And it worked. I was in control. Now the idea of leaving the house feels easy. Can you hear me, Mom?

MOM's voice is heard faintly through the phone, almost impossible for us to hear.

MOM: Yes, Morgan.

DANIEL: It's Daniel.

MOM: Is this Morgan?

DANIEL: No, Morgan is ... No, it's Daniel.

MOM: Oh dear, Morgan's waiting for me. He's in the woods.

DANIEL: Morgan's where? No, Mom; he's fine. Guess what, he's a counsellor now. How about that, huh? Crazy Morgan, giving advice. And still playing his music. He's doing great. He's fine.

MOM: We had the date wrong; camp is over. He's waiting to be picked up.

DANIEL: What? Waiting to be picked up? Oh, oh, no, that was when we were kids. You and Dad forgot to pick Morgan up from the Scout camp. Right, he was left waiting alone in the woods. We all had a good laugh about that. But that was a long time ago.

MOM: Tell Dad to pick him up.

DANIEL: No, Dad can't pick him up. He's dead.

MOM: Morgan died?

DANIEL: No, Mom. Dad. Dad's dead. He died years ago. Morgan's alive. He's fine. Please don't cry.

MOM: He's stranded. All alone … in the woods.

DANIEL: Listen to me. Morgan's not in the woods all alone. He's … not alone.

MOM: He thinks we don't love him.

DANIEL: He knows you love him.

MOM: I never got to say goodbye.

DANIEL: You'll get to say goodbye.

MOM: I'm sorry, Morgan …

DANIEL: It's Daniel, Mom. I'm coming to see you. Right now.

A BAR

MORGAN is still mid-song. Laughter can be heard as he continues.

MORGAN: (*to someone in the crowd*) Hey, up yours buddy. What? Oh, that's really mature. Right, well I actually used to sing professionally, so there. Forget it. This gig is over!!

Shift.

PHONE BOOTH

Rain. DANIEL stands in a phone booth. The blinking "Learn to Skydive" sign is reflected on the wet pavement. MORGAN walks along the street. MORGAN spots DANIEL in the phone booth.

MORGAN: Daniel? You're out! What are you doing in the phone booth?

DANIEL: Come in; you're getting soaked. I tried to visit Mom, but had a freak-out on my way there and couldn't make it any farther, so I ducked in here and I can't get out.

MORGAN squeezes into the phone booth.

MORGAN: Call a cab or something.

DANIEL: What's going on?

MORGAN: Daniel, am I old?

DANIEL: What?

MORGAN: I just got booed off stage.

DANIEL: With Hawk Rider?

MORGAN: No ... at karaoke ... by the ghost of Hawk Rider.

DANIEL: What?

MORGAN: I tried to get Hawk Rider back together ... everyone's got lives ... so I went to sing anyway ... because that's what I do. You know? I rock out. But in the crowd, this guy heckles me. Calls me Grandpa. Then I recognize him. He's the kid of our original bass player. He's in the bar! How did that happen?

DANIEL: I guess kids eventually grow up.

MORGAN: They thought I was a loser.

DANIEL: Don't take it so hard, Morgan. What do you care?

MORGAN: When I walked in, I felt like I was at home; they were singing all the old tunes, but not very well—no craftsmanship. So I thought I'd get up there and show them how it's really done. But when I tried, they just stared, looked embarrassed. Then I saw the mirror across the bar: there's a pathetic, middle-aged man onstage trying to do a high kick.

DANIEL: Oh, you didn't do the kicks, did you?

MORGAN: I feel like it all used to make sense. You know? There was a point when it was all clear. What happened to that?

DANIEL: Hey. Let's do your idea, let's go to the old campsite. Clear our heads.

MORGAN: Sure, Mr. Agrophobe. You can handle that.

DANIEL: Sure, Mr. Counsellor. Part of your program.

MORGAN: Yeah? Yeah! Maybe. A little extreme sports, to stimulate the soul.

DANIEL: Extreme sports? I suggested camping.

MORGAN: But how are we going to get to the site?

DANIEL: In Mom's Taurus?

MORGAN: And what's on the roof-rack Daniel?

DANIEL: Picnic basket?

MORGAN: That, an Adidas bag full of beer, and a couple of kayaks!

The sound of rushing water fills the space.

KAYAK

Shift. The two men are kayaking down raging rapids. MORGAN looks like he's having the time of his life. DANIEL is desperately trying to stay alive. MORGAN does a barrel roll and comes up beaming.

MORGAN: That wakes a guy up!

DANIEL: Fart, fart, fart.

DANIEL rolls over, but he can't right himself so he's going downstream with his head in the water. He burbles obscenities. Finally the kayak is righted, but he's lost his paddle.

MORGAN: What were you doing under there? Shampoo and rinse?

DANIEL's kayak has turned sideways so he's going down the rapids in profile.

MORGAN: Dude, point your boat forward.

DANIEL: I lost my paddle.

MORGAN: You gotta keep right here.

DANIEL: I don't have a paddle.

MORGAN: Dude, you've gotta take the right arm of this river or you're dead.

DANIEL: I don't have a paddle!

MORGAN: Bail out and swim.

DANIEL: Holy shit!!

DANIEL heads over a waterfall. Shift.

ASTRONOMY

Campfire at night. DANIEL wears a toque and sits by the campfire drying out.

MORGAN: That was some nice form you had going over the falls there.

DANIEL: I'm prone to ear infections.

MORGAN: You were way back in the seat—nice angle. Arms tucked tight to the chest. Near perfect ... except for not having a paddle. The kayak might show up downstream, too, you know. Lodged between some logs or something.

DANIEL: That's it?

MORGAN: That's what?

DANIEL: I almost get killed and you're worried about the kayak.

MORGAN: It's a rental.

DANIEL: A rental?

MORGAN: A rental.

Pause.

DANIEL: You know, Morgan, maybe the real problem is that you're a pathologically selfish human being.

This whole idea of helping me is just about helping you think you're more important than you actually are. Because ultimately you're just a narcissistic, arrogant prick, which is the reason why your roommate kicked you out, why your band broke up, why Mom had a breakdown because of the stress you caused her by your endless stupid pursuits that you guilt her into funding with never any thanks.

MORGAN: Mom didn't—

DANIEL: Look at you. Middle-aged and you're couch surfing, trying to sell your spurious skills to your own family members.

MORGAN: Mom called me to help *you* out, loser. Don't blame me for— Forget it. Maybe I should move out when we get home.

DANIEL: Ya think?

Awkward silence.

DANIEL: Let's just find that pact—get what we came for and get out of here.

MORGAN: Why bother. Probably long dissolved by now.

Awkward silence.

DANIEL: Wow. Lots of stars.

MORGAN: Oh yeah. Be nicer without that cloud covering up the middle.

DANIEL: That's the Milky Way.

MORGAN: Shit. Is it? Never see that in town.

DANIEL: No.

MORGAN: Beautiful.

DANIEL: Yeah. Really is.

Little lights illuminate on DANIEL's costume. He floats up and forms a constellation above MORGAN as the rest of the lights disappear. By shifting his limbs and rotating he becomes various recognizable constellations like Orion, and the Big Dipper.

MORGAN: I could never figure out the constellations. In Scouts I didn't get a badge because I called that the Big Dipper, but it was supposed to be the Big Bear. How do you get bear out of that?

Slowly, through this text, the OPERATORS are revealed manipulating the performers as they talk.

DANIEL: Remember those crazy conversations we used to have as kids?

MORGAN: We'd talk about aliens, black holes, and time travel.

DANIEL: Remember playing the game where we'd break our brains trying to conceive of the actual physical size of the universe?

MORGAN: Oh yeah. I loved pretending that the light bulb was a star for some microscopic universe. The dust particles were little planets with civilizations on them.

DANIEL: And then we'd imagine the reverse: that we were just on some little dust particle floating in some kid's room. Or we were some experiment in some laboratory being observed by these beings so big that there wasn't any math that could represent them.

MORGAN: How's that ear?

DANIEL: Full of bacteria.

MORGAN: Come here.

They drift closer together. MORGAN puts his arm around DANIEL.

MORGAN: Share the heat—it's an old Scout trick.

DANIEL: I'll bet it is. Scouter Rick probably taught you this one.

MORGAN: Scouter Rick and Scouter Greg saved me from hypothermia in Whitehorse.

DANIEL: In their tent.

MORGAN: Yep.

DANIEL: A little Scout sandwich.

MORGAN: Yeah.

DANIEL: Pervs. (*beat*) What's it like?

MORGAN: What? A Scout sandwich?

DANIEL: The moment you let go of the plane.

MORGAN: It's the anti-choice. The action that defies everything your body thinks it wants. Safety. Security. And instead it goes for what it really needs. Trust. But I don't mean trust as in trust in the parachute or technology, but rather trust that your life is your life, and existence is yours alone—and it's bigger than Earth, bigger than time. And all you ever have is you.

DANIEL: Sounds lonely. I really hope we find that pact out here.

MORGAN: When we would have those late-night conversations, you'd always fall asleep ahead of me. I'd be riffing on some whacked-out philosophical question, acting like I knew all the answers, and eventually I'd realize I was talking to myself.

You'd have just drifted off in the middle of my lecture. When that would happen, I'd imagine that you had already made it to tomorrow. You know how sleep goes by instantaneously—one second you're lying in the dark talking, and the next you're opening your eyes to the smell of bacon or the sound of news on the radio. So I would assume, for you, the night had already passed. I'd have been left behind in yesterday—alone in the dark, and you were already awake, safe in the sunlight of morning. Daniel?

Deep breathing of sleep.

MORGAN: Alone again.

Lights fade away. A ticking travel clock. More snoring.

SUBTERRANEAN MEN'S ROOM

Darkness. Water running. An eerie light.

DANIEL: Are you there?

MORGAN: Where are we? What's with all these urinals? This place is disgusting.

Some more light. Dripping.

DANIEL: I recognize it.

MORGAN: God, I'm so confused. What are we—

DANIEL: Oh. I know this place. This is a dream environment that I'm often in.

MORGAN: Dream environment?

Both guys quickly look at their hands, then check their watches, look away, then look back again, register surprise. When they look up, they discover that MORGAN is floating.

MORGAN: Oh shit. I'm dreaming.

DANIEL's head starts to head for the floor—his standard lucid dream position.

DANIEL: Me too. Oh crap, crap, crap.

MORGAN: Look at you. Loser. I am so going to rip you when we wake up.

DANIEL: When we wake up? Oh my god! Morgan, we're doing it.

MORGAN: Doing what? What are we doing?

DANIEL: We're really doing it. We're in the same dream.

MORGAN: Same dream?

DANIEL: Oh, Morgan, do you grasp what is happening to us right now? This is the dreamer's holy grail. We've breeched some sort of threshold, crossed the barrier of our individual egos!

MORGAN: Wait a minute, wait a minute, wait a minute. Just wait a minute, Daniel! How the hell is this happening? How can we be sharing the same dream?

DANIEL: Don't stress—your dream mind doesn't work like your waking mind, so you'll only frustrate yourself trying to figure it out.

MORGAN: Ha. Got it. I'm just dreaming that we're sharing the same dream. You're just a dream version of you.

DANIEL: Are you lucid?

MORGAN: I think so.

DANIEL: So if I'm only your dream, you could make me disappear. Turn me into something else.

MORGAN concentrates like he's casting a spell. Lights flicker. Go out. Thunderclap. When the lights restore, DANIEL is still there, but he's now wearing a long blonde wig.

DANIEL: What the hell did you do?

MORGAN: I tried to turn you into Angelina Jolie.

DANIEL: She doesn't have blonde hair.

MORGAN: In my dreams she does.

DANIEL: Well, it appears we have somewhat limited control over each other. But I'm still here, so that should prove that we're sharing the dream.

MORGAN: No, that is totally impossible.

DANIEL: Look around; do you recognize this place?

MORGAN: No.

DANIEL: Well, I do.

MORGAN: So you're saying this is your dream?

DANIEL: No, it's our dream.

DANIEL gestures to the wig.

DANIEL: It contains elements of both our minds.

MORGAN: I can't wake up. What if we're stuck in here forever?! I can't breathe.

DANIEL: Relax, we'll be okay. I'm here; you're safe. There's probably a logical way out. We'll just find the exit.

MORGAN is still freaked.

MORGAN: All right then. If this is your dream environment, where do we go?

DANIEL: I suggest we go that way. There's usually a sort of mall-ish, hotel-like convention centre complex just past the row of backed-up toilets being plunged by that janitor. However, be careful; I often end up naked right about now.

MORGAN: Great.

Horror music. Footsteps. Menacing plunging sounds. MORGAN pulls DANIEL close and whispers.

MORGAN: That janitor looks a lot like Charles Manson.

DANIEL: I agree; but it's the only path through. Okay, listen, on my signal we'll make a break for it: you head for the door—the code on the keypad is eight-six ... seven-five-three ... zero ... nine.

MORGAN: Eight-six-seven-five-three-oh-nine?

DANIEL: Eight-six-seven, five-three-oh-nine.

MORGAN: (*as if trying to memorize it, only vaguely aware that there's something familiar about the numbers*) Eight-six-seven-five-three-oh-ni-ee-ine.

DANIEL: On the other side, you go down the hall, take a left and through the big industrial kitchen with all the *Iron Chef* competitors; just past there there's a lobby-slash-operating room where the patients are usually those M&M characters. Avoid looking, because it's not a peanut inside the big one. Just keep going and I'll meet you in the elevator with the glass doors and the two little girls from *The Shining.* Don't worry; I've made friends with them.

MORGAN: Yeah, but what about Charlie?

MORGAN makes a psycho slashing gesture with his hand.

DANIEL: I'll distract him.

MORGAN: How are you going to distract him?

DANIEL tosses his long blonde hair in a confident, sexy, Charlie's Angels *kind of way, and speaks in a tough-guy, action-hero tone.*

DANIEL: I'll think of something.

Pause.

MORGAN: You know, I really really want to wake up now.

DANIEL: The elevator. Go. Helter Skelter!

The men split up and do a series of action hero gestures running across space, jumping, sliding, doing cartwheels. A sort of Matrix-*like display of super cool movement to music that's a hybrid of theme songs from* Magnum, P.I. *and* The A-Team.

ELEVATOR

Suddenly there's elevator Muzak. The men ride calmly up. They search the button panel.

MORGAN: Press "G" for Ground or, better yet, see if there's an "A" for Awake.

DANIEL: I can't find that.

MORGAN: Wow, this must be a tall building; look at these numbers. They're in the thousands.

DANIEL: No look; these numbers aren't floors—they're years.

(*He points at the buttons.*) 1976, 1994, 2002 …

MORGAN: Oh, let's go to 2112. I want to see what it's like in the future. Plus, it's my favourite album by Rush.

DANIEL: It's locked off.

MORGAN: They're all locked. Except this one. 1992.

DANIEL: What happened in 1992?

A bell rings. The elevator doors open and the men get out.

FUNERAL HOME

Music: a church organ plays. It's a funeral. DANIEL and MORGAN are at the back of the funeral chapel.

MORGAN: Oh. That 1992.

DANIEL: It's Dad's funeral. We have travelled back in time.

MORGAN: I don't want to relive this funeral. It was horrible.

DANIEL: Morgan, maybe that's the point. Maybe this is our chance to put things right. We're in control.

MORGAN: What are you planning on doing?

DANIEL: I'm going to the viewing.

MORGAN: No. He looks horrible. The undertaker botched the job.

DANIEL: I know. And I was too upset, too frightened to face him, and so I never really said goodbye. That was wrong. I'm going in. Are you coming?

MORGAN: I'm scared.

DANIEL: Just stay present; we're in control here.

They enter the viewing room and approach the coffin. MORGAN can't look.

DANIEL: Dad. Dad?

MORGAN: How does he look?

DANIEL: He's not even here. It's just full of paper.

MORGAN: (*looks*) What is it?

DANIEL: Weird, it's all Greyhound bus tickets.

MORGAN: I can't quite hold on to the text. Where are they for?

DANIEL: Does that say Missouri or Mississauga?

MORGAN: I think it says "Missing."

DANIEL: Where's Missing? What's that supposed to mean?

MORGAN: Well, Dad's missing from his coffin. Maybe that's—hey, this coffin is leaking.

DANIEL: It's flooding the whole chapel!

MORGAN: We're going to drown!

DANIEL: We've got to get out of here. Fast!

MORGAN: I've got it! We're in a church. Perfect place for a *deus ex machina*! I'll just call God and he and/or she will save us.

DANIEL: You're not even religious. Why don't we just try to generate a jet-ski or something?

MORGAN: How do we do this?

He clasps his hands together.

MORGAN: Dear Santa …

Suddenly, a spotlight hits MORGAN. He looks up.

MORGAN: God?

Music. A choir of angels. Daniel looks around confused. Shift.

HIGH SCHOOL PAGEANT

Music. A classic pop song, such as Madonna's "Like A Prayer," plays.

DANIEL: What the hell …? Hey, Morgan? Morgan. Morgan, do you hear singing like:

MORGAN lip-synchs to the music.

DANIEL: This is so inappropriate.

Another spotlight picks out DANIEL. A flash of recognition crosses his face as the dance rhythm kicks in.

DANIEL: Oh god, no.

He's compelled by unknown forces to accompany his brother with spontaneous back-up choreography.

DANIEL: (*whispers desperately*) Morgan.

Break. Rushing wind. DANIEL is falling. A moment of horror. Restore.

During the song's chorus, DANIEL grabs MORGAN and herds him to the edge of the stage.

DANIEL: What is this?

MORGAN: High school lip-synch finals: 1989.

DANIEL: We're further back in time.

MORGAN: This is the one time Dad came to one of my things.

DANIEL: And you were booed by him.

MORGAN: Now I'm gonna get it right. With choreography.

DANIEL: No, Morgan. I can't do this. Please. Ah, shit.

He sings. DANIEL's sucked back into the choreography. The two men hold hands as they dance.

DANIEL: I'm humiliated.

Back-up dancers appear from the darkness and take the chorus. As they sing and dance, DANIEL exclaims to MORGAN:

DANIEL: Hey, I'm a pretty good dancer! That guy's giving us a standing ovation.

MORGAN: He's not cheering. He's screaming. Look at his hands. He's got the astigmatism!

DANIEL: Stigmata.

MORGAN: Whatever, his hands are bleeding and he's rushing the stage. Run!

DANIEL: Where?

MORGAN: There's a window behind the judges' table. Can you get to it?

DANIEL: They're in the way.

MORGAN: You could jump over.

DANIEL: How?

MORGAN: Flashdance!

A dance break. DANIEL discovers he's wearing a pair of leg warmers. He does a desperate attempt at some high-impact aerobics, culminating in him pulling off Jennifer Beals' triumphant running dive roll for the dance-school audition panel. The sound of breaking glass. DANIEL has gone through the window and is falling. He recovers and lands in a dark environment.

Shift.

NINJA

Creepy music.

MORGAN: Where are we now?

DANIEL: Isn't this our street from our first house?

MORGAN: In Summerland.

DANIEL: Lousy Okanagan.

MORGAN: We're further back in time.

DANIEL: Look: broken eggs.

MORGAN: Oh, this is that night we went and egged Darren's house.

DANIEL: And we accidentally hit that freaky goth dude who was always wandering alone downtown.

MORGAN: Jarvis.

DANIEL: Jarvis. Egg all over his trench coat.

MORGAN: It was an accident.

DANIEL: And he jumped you.

MORGAN: I'll pay to get it cleaned.

DANIEL: Started smacking you.

MORGAN: He's gonna kill me.

DANIEL: He pulled a knife.

MORGAN: Help, Daniel!

DANIEL: But I just stood and watched. I couldn't move. So helpless, useless; so scared I just left my body—frozen like a dream.

MORGAN: And for months I would find you hiding in your room, posing in front of the mirror, Taekwon-Do magazines lying at your feet ...

DANIEL: Because I wanted a replay of that night. Give him this:

> DANIEL jumps up and gives MORGAN a flying front snap-kick to the face.

MORGAN: Yeah! Nice! And how about one of these:

MORGAN gives DANIEL an elbow to the throat and a head-butt. They continue to pummel each other with super-hero moves. Until they scream together:

TOGETHER: I just want to kill him!

They do one more huge flying kick. Wind rushes. They're falling. DANIEL is pulling at his costume desperately, helplessly; he lands somewhere. MORGAN drops beside him.

THE RAVINE

A gentle breeze. DANIEL and MORGAN are looking over the edge of a vast ravine.

MORGAN: We're at the ravine.

DANIEL: We weren't allowed to play here.

MORGAN: We'd be grounded forever.

DANIEL: But we snuck here that one time, to throw the parachute guys off the cliff.

DANIEL: Shhh. Listen. Voices.

MORGAN: Where?

DANIEL: Look, down there, on the path. There's a couple of kids.

MORGAN: Oh no, creepy kids on their own. That's always a bad sign. Go away, go away, go away; I turn you into chocolate cake.

DANIEL: They're heading towards the cliff.

MORGAN: So?

DANIEL: Well, look at the drop-off; it's not safe. (*calling out*) Hey!

MORGAN: What are you doing?

DANIEL: Hey, kids!

MORGAN: Shhh. Don't attract their attention. They might be possessed, or evil, or "of the corn."

DANIEL: Hey! Up here!

DANIEL waves, then stops short.

DANIEL: Morgan … Do you recognize those kids?

MORGAN: No.

DANIEL: Look harder.

Beat.

MORGAN: Holy—Daniel.

DANIEL: I know.

MORGAN: It's us.

DANIEL: Now I remember.

The men perform the voices of their younger selves who are represented by little action figures controlled by an unseen puppeteer.

DANIEL: I want to be able to fly.

MORGAN: Be a pilot?

DANIEL: No, just really fly. You can't, but maybe when we grow up they'll have, like, jet packs or something.

MORGAN: I know how we can fly.

As adults.

DANIEL: And that was the moment. That was when we made the pact. Promised we'd do it and that we'd never let each other down.

MORGAN: It was ... I thought it happened somewhere else, but it was here.

DANIEL: And then we let our parachute guys go and the wind took them and we followed them down the side of the cliff to the bottom of the ravine. Had to crawl through the underbrush, all the tangled bushes, a place where nobody would ever get to, and then ...

As kids.

MORGAN: Look.

DANIEL: What is it?

MORGAN: It's a boot. A leg ... It's a person under there. Danny, it's Jarvis.

DANIEL: What's he doing? Is he asleep?

MORGAN: No. Daniel, he's dead.

DANIEL: I'm scared.

MORGAN: He fell. Or jumped. Or something ...

DANIEL: We better get someone.

MORGAN: No! Are you crazy? How can we know about him if we've never been here?

DANIEL: But we *are* here.

MORGAN: Yeah, but if Dad finds out, we'll be grounded for life.

DANIEL: But he's dead; we have to—

MORGAN: And what if they think we killed him?

DANIEL: We can't just—

MORGAN: Listen! You're not going to tell. This never happened. Got it? We were never here. We never saw this. You have to promise me.

DANIEL: But he's—

MORGAN: Are you going to take his side again, like that night in the park?

DANIEL: I didn't—

MORGAN: Who do you care about? Him or me?

DANIEL: Morgan ...

MORGAN: Then promise.

DANIEL: I promise.

MORGAN: Sign it.

DANIEL: (*as adult*) And we wrote it on the paper under the skydive promise. And you used your Scout knife, so sharp you got a badge for it, and told me to cut you.

MORGAN: And you cut me.

DANIEL: And then you took it back.

MORGAN: And cut you.

DANIEL: And we pressed our palms to the paper.

MORGAN: Signed in blood.

DANIEL: And we didn't tell.

MORGAN: What's that sound? Daniel?

DANIEL: They put up posters. Missing. His face, a yearbook photo, yellowing on telephone poles, in arcades and Greyhound bus depots. And still we never said.

MORGAN: There are rocks falling ... Danny it's a landslide!

DANIEL: Those posters! Years, Morgan. For years. Computer aging, this is what he'd look like now. Except there is no now. Only then. And we knew it and said nothing.

MORGAN: Shit, Danny ... I think this whole slope is going to give.

DANIEL: And that kid's family—and he was just a kid, sixteen, maybe— didn't know, never knew, what had happened to him ...

MORGAN: We're in trouble!

DANIEL: What do you think that is like? Not knowing what happened to someone you love. Wondering if they're alive or dead or in pain or crying for you somewhere dark and far away.

MORGAN: Daniel, I don't want to die in here. They say if you die dreaming, you really die!

DANIEL: And it was then we started to drift apart. The pact became a promise to forget.

MORGAN: Daniel, help me!

Sound of thundering rocks, the cliff crumbling around them. Light is growing.

DANIEL: Okay, time's up. It's morning. Let's go.

MORGAN: Where?

DANIEL: Look down. Can you see?

MORGAN: It's us. Right now. Asleep!

DANIEL: Yes. Dive straight down. Aim for your own chest. You've got to drive yourself right back into your body to wake up.

MORGAN: It's a long way down.

DANIEL: It's the only way. There's nothing left to hang on to up here.

MORGAN: Okay.

DANIEL grabs his hand.

DANIEL: On three. One, two …

MORGAN: Daniel, I remember …

DANIEL: Three.

They dive down. A crashing, tearing, roaring sound.

FALSE AWAKENING

DANIEL and MORGAN wake up in the cabin. A mosquito buzzes. DANIEL slaps his face. The mosquito continues to buzz.

DANIEL: Mosquitoes. Morgan?

MORGAN: Danny?

DANIEL: Yeah.

MORGAN: You awake?

DANIEL: Yeah. You?

MORGAN: Woah … Danny?

DANIEL: Yeah, Morgan.

MORGAN swats a mosquito.

MORGAN: Danny, did we …?

DANIEL: We did.

MORGAN: The dream?

DANIEL: Yeah.

MORGAN: How?

DANIEL: I don't know.

MORGAN: Danny, I'm sorry.

DANIEL: I know. I was in your brain.

MORGAN: You were.

DANIEL: And you were in mine.

Pause.

MORGAN: What now?

DANIEL: Paratherapy.

MORGAN: For you?

DANIEL: For us.

MORGAN: Yeah?

DANIEL: Yeah. I want to fulfil the destiny, our destiny.

MORGAN: Oh yeah!

They perform a riff of air guitar.

MORGAN: What a trip!

DANIEL: I know!

MORGAN: You look fantastic!

DANIEL: Thank you.

MORGAN: You're floating.

DANIEL: That's how I feel.

MORGAN: No, you're really floating.

Beat of recognition. DANIEL's head drifts towards the floor.

DANIEL: Uh ...

MORGAN: Oh ... Shit ...

DANIEL: Morgan ... We're not out yet.

MORGAN: But we're back where we started, right?

DANIEL: Or did we start somewhere else?

Beat.

DANIEL: What happened?

MORGAN: We tried to snap you out of your funk.

DANIEL: Paratherapy.

MORGAN: Karaoke.

DANIEL: Kayaking.

MORGAN: Camping.

DANIEL: We shared a dream.

MORGAN: Woke up.

DANIEL: Made up.

MORGAN: We agreed to jump. (*pause*) And we went home.

DANIEL: I remember.

MORGAN: We trained.

DANIEL: You taught me the positions.

MORGAN: We registered.

DANIEL: Picked our chutes.

MORGAN: We flew to the spot.

DANIEL: And we jumped.

MORGAN: Damn mosquito!

DANIEL: And it was fantastic, and we almost touched, but we didn't; we ran out of time, so I pulled my cord ... and ...and ...

MORGAN: Driving me crazy ...

DANIEL: Morgan, that's not a mosquito ...

MORGAN: What is it?

DANIEL: Look.

> *The buzzing object is revealed to be a tiny plane drifting away. Plane engine receding. Music.*

THE CRASH

> *A roar of wind, loud, then louder, then deafening, then silence. We return to the moment when DANIEL's chute doesn't open. Stillness.*

MORGAN: Have you ever been in a really bad accident? Then you know that feeling where you can think in long, complicated sentences, while at the same time act instinctively without thought or language. Funny, in the moment, I could imagine telling the story of this day even as I lived it at a speed too fast for words. I remember. This is what happened. Or rather this is what is happening right now. We make eye contact—I know his chute isn't functioning. I know it. It did not happen all too fast to know, because I know it; and I pull my chute anyway.

DANIEL: (*whispers*) Help me.

> *MORGAN pulls.*

MORGAN: And instantly he's a pinprick, a speck, a fleck among the greens and greys below. That's how fast he's falling as I slow down under the drag of my opening chute.

DANIEL is gone.

MORGAN: Now I have, at the exact same time, four lines of thought running through my head: "Pull your reserve, Dan; pull your reserve, Dan; pull your reserve, Dan; pull your reserve, Dan …"

The line loops.

MORGAN: That's the first line. Then there was, "I could catch him. If I release now, I could catch him. I have no time, but if I go now, I might still catch him …"

The line loops on top of first.

MORGAN: That's two; then there was a third. "What am I going to tell Mom?"

The line loops on top of first two.

MORGAN: Then the fourth. "It all happened too fast. It all happened too fast. It all happened too fast. It all happened too fast."

Shift.

MORGAN: BUT IT DID NOT HAPPEN TOO FAST!

DANIEL: Pull, pull, pull, pull, pull …

MORGAN: And then, HOLY SHIT, I pull. I release the main chute and fall diving head down. He's impossibly far; the earth is impossibly near. I'm certain that this is death, but as I close in on him with the ground looming larger, I begin to think.

DANIEL: You can do this.

MORGAN: I can see him clearly now. His body is limp and tumbling, pummelled by the air resistance. I think, "How the hell am I going to hang on to that?"

DANIEL: And then ...

MORGAN: Boom! We collide. I bounce off of him, then reach for him—

DANIEL: —catch a piece of clothing—

MORGAN: —then lose it. Then I get a—

DANIEL: —foot in the face!

MORGAN: Do a back-flip and see the ground. It's coming fast.

DANIEL: Hand in the face, a kick in the gut.

MORGAN: My goggles are knocked off and sort of just hang by my head in a really annoying way for the next ten feet as my eyes are stretched in the wind, filling with tears. I feel my way back to my brother.

DANIEL: Grab him.

MORGAN: Hold him. Force him into position.

DANIEL: An embrace.

MORGAN: And I look down and—

DANIEL: Snapshot!

MORGAN: The earth—so close that I can see the finer details. The highway beneath us, the individual cars, a hitchhiker in a breezy skirt, I can see her hippie boyfriend hiding behind an electrical box in the ditch, waiting to hop out when a car stopped for the sexy single girl trap. I hate that hippie! How close are we? How much distance do we need to slow down?

DANIEL: Five hundred metres.

MORGAN: That's all we need?

DANIEL: No. We need seven-fifty. Five hundred is what we've got.

MORGAN: Only five hundred, eh?

DANIEL: Four-fifty now.

MORGAN: Somehow we're wrapped around each other and I free a hand to pull the reserve.

DANIEL: His hand is fumbling, crawling across the fabric.

MORGAN: Come on!

DANIEL: Four hundred metres.

MORGAN: I can't feel … my fingers are flopping around like a rubber glove with nothing inside it.

DANIEL: Three-fifty.

MORGAN: I catch hold of something and pull.

DANIEL: That's the strap to my freakin' helmet, dude!

MORGAN: Which instantly flies off and hits me in the face. Shit! I reach again.

DANIEL: Three hundred!

MORGAN: Something, something, anything.

DANIEL: Pull!

MORGAN: I pull.

DANIEL: Two-fifty!

MORGAN: In the reflection in Daniel's eyes I can see the chute flowing out behind me, all white and fluid. And then I see …

DANIEL: Two hundred.

MORGAN: The chute starts to fill with air.

DANIEL: One-fifty.

MORGAN: And there's a sudden horrible pull as it begins to drag. Daniel's grip slips and there's absolutely no way I can hold him with these rubber-glove hands. He's gone! But no—he's there. His harness is caught on mine and now he's dangling around my legs and I'm grabbing at his head and shoulders.

DANIEL: One hundred metres from the ground.

MORGAN: I can't control the safety-chute, and we're spinning erratically as we decelerate. It's like somebody dropped a Tilt-A-Whirl from the CN Tower.

DANIEL: Eighty metres.

MORGAN: And we're still going way too fast.

DANIEL: Sixty metres.

MORGAN: And I need to brace myself for the impact.

DANIEL: Fifty metres.

MORGAN: We're heading for some trees.

DANIEL: Forty metres.

MORGAN: I can't do metric. What's that in feet?

DANIEL: Hundred and sixty! Fifty. Forty. Thirty.

MORGAN's lines overlap as DANIEL counts down the distance.

MORGAN: I grab the lines and pull hard.

DANIEL: One-twenty! One-ten. One hundred.

MORGAN: The chute buckles, spins, but it's too late; we hit the top of the trees at about ninety feet.

TOGETHER: Arms and legs and branches and twigs, and—

MORGAN: —for a brief moment—

DANIEL: —fingers.

MORGAN: Something snaps, tears, catches, flips. And I hang upside down in the air—the weight of Daniel's body is, is where … is … gone.

DANIEL: Snap.

MORGAN: And then I drop head first twenty feet to the ground.

DANIEL: Blackout.

Blackout.

A NIGHTMARE

Sound of hospital in the darkness.

MORGAN is asleep.

DANIEL: At night he is alone. Like all of us are alone. Like in that way that everyone dies alone, everyone sleeps alone. And like everyone, he just disappears into that very vulnerable crab-shell of a body and sleeps that defenceless, helpless sleep.

Figures emerge from the dark. They begin to manipulate MORGAN, who continues to sleep.

DANIEL: In his dreams, he his spoken of in the third person. Numerous mumbling voices at the edge of darkness observe him. In this dream he is the subject of an experiment.

He is laid out on a gurney or operating table.

DANIEL: He is being dissected—slowly dismembered—while alive. And he can't communicate. That was the first thing they took out. The voice box. It's on a little table—he can almost see it; it's a little black box like the kind in an airplane—but fleshy and wet. It contains the important information. The clues about this thing, this body—its flight path and

92

trajectory—and distress signals. But it's out and gone and he is absolutely silent as the dark voices continue to mumble and move around on the edge of the light and observe and judge his condition. They take off his limbs. They sew his legs where his arms should be and his arms are sewn on to the ends of his legs. He now has leg-arms. Which means if you want to hold something, you have to kick it first— which is tough because then it's usually gone or broken by the time your hands get it. And if you want to walk away you have to cup the road in your hands and bring it up to your feet and lay it out to walk on. And maybe you've messed the road up and it's now going somewhere else. Fuckin' leg-arms. And the voices keep mumbling. And they shave his head—put the hair in a cereal bowl, all cottony and mixed up. And with a black felt marker they draw lines on his head. A map of where they want to go next. They mumble, draw, mumble, draw. The marker squeaks out their intentions—and we all speak magic marker at least a little bit, and he gets the gist of what they're up to.

Lights fade away from MORGAN and the surgeons as they seem to be transferring him from the operating table to somewhere else.

DANIEL: He feels the coming invasion. The place where the thoughts are taken apart. Where there is no understanding.

And all the ideas are cut up and dropped down sewers, stuffed in the bottom of a box in the unfinished basement, put in the boiler room of the condemned high school, and under the stage, and in the crawl spaces and in the folds and crevasses and holes and cracks that are too dark and small to even know, and all those thoughts are as lonely as sleep. And nothing is known anymore. And all that's left is the horrible suspicion that something has been lost.

Lights fade to black.

DANIEL: Wake up.

Shift.

AWAKENING

MORGAN emerges from the darkness in a wheelchair. He checks his watch, looks away. Checks again. He sighs and, facing downstage, he holds his head for a moment. From the darkness, DANIEL appears behind him. MORGAN looks up, but can't see him as he's directly behind.

MORGAN: Danny?

DANIEL: Yes.

MORGAN: I've been dreaming about you.

DANIEL: Oh yeah?

MORGAN: I wake up—it's like a night terror. Something sitting on my chest—I can't move; I know I'm still half asleep, body frozen with the dream.

DANIEL: It's time you wake right up then.

MORGAN: I kinda wanna stay in.

DANIEL: But you can't, can you?

MORGAN: No. (*pause*) Daniel?

DANIEL: Yeah?

MORGAN: It's like those nights when we were kids. You've slipped ahead into morning, somewhere unknown, and I'm left behind again, just stuck in darkness.

DANIEL: Yeah?

MORGAN: And I'm lying here, wondering how to catch up.

DANIEL: Mmm-hmm.

MORGAN: What do I do?

DANIEL: Well, back then, even in the middle of the night, I was always there, wasn't I? Asleep, dreaming of the day before while you lay awake thinking of day ahead.

MORGAN: Yeah.

DANIEL: Look up. Stars are out tonight. See us flying?

NIGHT SKY

MORGAN takes hold of his wheels and turns his chair upstage to see DANIEL, but as he turns, DANIEL floats up into the space above. Music plays and DANIEL flies free above MORGAN, who wheels among the machinery. Stars fill the sky, with DANIEL floating among the constellations. MORGAN looks up into the sky at the stars.

Fade to black.